# Like Aliens
# Hitching a Ride
# On Human Brains

©Copyright Jacqueline Howard 2018

## Author Jacqueline Howard

Caution: "F' words, and the "B" words.  A Lot of Swearing is present, in this short story, and poetic, yet dramatic, situations. (Added Photography, some double, to inspire your Mind, and Empty pages, for you, to write, your, 'Alien') thoughts in☺.  Perhaps.

I was going, to Title this short story, 'Like Aliens Fucking Your Brains' ☺

Therefore, I decided, to not offend everyone, just the 'Alien entity' and those possessed, by its source, and carried on fucking up, the 'Alien entity's Brain'!

Those who know me, know that, they never, hear me swear!  Only 'a slip' one'.

Therefore, it came to my attention, too many people are walking around, not knowing, their Brains, have been, invaded by, the 'Alien entity'.

A lot of people, like to swear, and do not realise, how much power, it is giving, the 'Alien entity'.

The energy, it creates, gives off, a signal, and the 'Alien entity', attaches, to its vibration frequency, so to speak!

If you know, what I mean.  It is the plug-in point, as you are the power, they need, to plug into!

Whatever way, you generate it, they will hitch, a ride into your brains, and then, they have hooked, into you.

Alien abduction is common & most times, they will return you back, to your body.

However, you will never be, the same again.  Sometimes, they never return you, and then you are, on the other side, invisible, as in Spirit/Alien form.

Until they decide to reappear again.  Some people remind you, of someone, you know, don't they?

Have you ever wondered why?

We do not know much, about what happens, on the other side of life, but there is something remarkable, that makes one person, look so similar, to another.

Yet they have no ancestors, in common, with one another, at all!

The invisible source, produces similar features, and people start to look similar, to another person.  Sometimes, we mistake someone, that looks like, someone else.

Perhaps, it's due to the, 'Spirit/Alien connection'.

We originated, from the Alien entity, and that is what, they have in common, with human earthlings.

Sometimes, giving a shit about someone, or something, lands you, in mischief, and unnecessary, dramatic situations.

Life is full of the 'F' words.  If you have been touched, by an 'Alien' source, you will know, they love to hear you swear, and thrive, on its powerful energy, that it, gives them.

(You never, swear much, prior, until you realise, if you cannot beat them, join them).  And that is, what they like!

Oppose them, and you are, on your own.

They will, use the brain, of other people, to go against you! Simple, but true!

You try hard, and do not get anywhere.  Because, they are working, against you.

After all, the facts, are proof, to you!

Get close, to your opposition, and you will soon, find out, who is jealous, and not going, to allow you, to be successful.

However, you do not care, so you do what you enjoy, and 'Fuck the rest'!  Right?

In time, that is what eventuates out of all, your hard work!

For example, some people, do not know, an Alien, has touched them.

That is, until after the 'Zapping' or the so-called 'Shock', after effects has taken place.

How do you know, if an 'Alien', has touched, someone?

You cannot miss it.  The person, will always leave you, feeling upset, about something, or about someone, or upset you, whichever way, swear words, can get, the message through, a lot faster.

You can also, suspect them, when the other person, takes on your role.  They want, to be, like you.

They want to try to do better than you do.

They want, to make you think, they are doing better, than you are.

They do not like it, when you are in love, with someone, or in love, with something, you like.

They will try, to tell you, it is not good, and they will make you think, they are always right, and they will tell you, they are right, because, things went wrong, for you.

They are making things, go wrong, because, they are thinking, and hoping, you do not succeed, in what you like.

They hope your relationship, falls apart, and they are, the only ones, that can brag, about their so-called, good relationship.

They will also tell you, they have been, in bad relationship and, advise you, to not bother, being, in any relationship.

They will, want you, to have nothing, go right for you, so they can have power, over you.

'That's because, of the Alien entity, that is, with them, and fucking with, their brains'.  Because, that is how, the 'Alien entity', gets to fuck, with your brains, too.

They will not let you, suspect, it's them.  They will always be there, to remind you, they are there for you, if you need them.

 Because, they know, and hope, you will need them.  If you did not need them around, they will have, a major panic attack, and begin to lose power, of control, over your life.

That is, what they, do not want, to see happen.  Therefore, they keep thinking, and hoping things, go wrong, for you, because, that way, you will need, them around.  Get the picture?

This is how 'The Alien entity' works their way, around you. Through people, you know.

Through people, you least suspect, because, you would not think, they are possessed, by an 'Alien.

They, themselves, do not, always know, it's happening. One day, they will realise, they are thinking things, that are not right for you, and for, them.

They should be wishing, the best for you, and not acting like, an overbearing protective, possessive, personality.

'The Alien entity' makes them behave that way, without them knowing.

One day they discover, they are on their own, with this 'Alien entity' and have to figure out, how to deal, with their possessive, personality.

At some point, they will turn, to someone else, and behave that way, with them, because, you are not there for them.

While the 'Alien entity', is in their mind, and fucking with their brains, it will interfere, with your plans.

If you make it known, you do not have time, for them, and that you are happy, with what you are doing.

'The Alien entity', will know, you are not available, for the 'Alien entity', to fuck with your mind, and your plans.

Taking back control, takes effort and determination.

'The Alien entity' already is aware, of your vulnerable side, to what you want, and need, and will play, against you, if you let it.

Temptation, is big business to 'The Alien entity'. Remember, 'The Alien' plays, to win. ☺

They do not care, if you lose friends, money, or jobs, along the way.  They only are here, to learn, and win, at whatever cost.

If they lose, they also lose power of control, over you, and cannot fuck with your brains.

However, they will wait, until they see, you have a weakness, and try fucking with your brains, again.

They will use, other people, and other sources, to gain their power, of control, over you.

You can match them, with as many swear words, as you like.  Making them, have so much power, while you keep swearing.

Alternatively, you can laugh, when you swear, and the energy, from those words, will shift, because you added laughter to it.

You give out, the laughter vibration energy, to them, which is not the same as, the serious energy, which carries more weight.

Words have power, especially the 'F & B' words.  The 'Fucking word, and the 'Bitch and Bastard' words, all carry a source of energy, that transmits power, to the 'Alien source'.

You can also decide, to view this story, as a 'Make-believe' that would make, a great powerful, big blockbuster, Movie.

Yes, imagine watching it, on the big screen, in the cinema. (With a lot of fucking, swear words)!  The more swearing, the better, the movie looks.  (The Aliens, love it, & seem to thrive on that energy source).

I will discuss this, as we go deep into, the story.

Anyway, we shall see, if they require, my assistance, to brainwash, the 'Alien source', into serving me.

 It will, not be easy, as they already know, I am aware, of their existence.

I would have to hypnotize, 'the aliens', and they will then, be under, my command, only for a short time, while the Movie, is being made.. (the mind, creates, the movie, right?) ☺

The 'Alien' thrives on power.  Humans, have what they need, to keep the 'Alien world, and its source, fully charged. They transmit, receive, transfer, and become Mutants, without you, realising it.

Sad to say, they do not like you, when you discover 'The Alien power source' and they further, do not like you, discovering them.  Being invisible, makes them, powerful.

Unless, you become aware of it, and their presence, that is when they begin, to turn things, against you, and use, other people, to do so.

Have you, wondered why, you feel unlucky, jinxed, or betrayed, or whatever you do, somehow, something gets in the way of it?

No doubt, you did not, suspect, 'The Alien source' connecting, to people, to cause their brains, to be, fucked with.

Yes, they are fucking, with human brains, anyway they can, to get, a power boost.  Aliens thrive, on that power of energy boost, it gives them.  Without it, they are weak, and drained, of the powerful energy.

Their world, and ours, can only get along, through transfer, of power, from one world, to another.

'If you say 'Fuck You' to someone, think about, how it makes you feel, and then think about, how it makes the other person feel.

You will get, a clear indication, through their response, to how much power, is being transmitted, to the 'Alien' source.

If they get, fully charged up. 'Aliens' love, to take over, a person, and remain 'Like they are the Boss', and have control, over you.

After all, you are like a source of food to them. Just like, Food is Power to the human body, and like such, your words carry powerful energy, to 'The Alien source'.

Whatever makes them thrive, will help them, remain feeding, of that power source. In addition, believe it or not, 'Humans' have, what they need.

'Believe it or Not', The 'Alien entity', can even penetrate, the mind, of the animal. Animals behaving strangely, especially when an 'Alien entity', is around you.

Why do dogs bark? Have they, been zapped too? In addition, touched by an 'Alien entity'?

You might as well, believe whatever you like, at this stage.

Alternatively, be very observant, to the 'maybe' is possible, and could be, a probable occurrence.

Anyway, to be prepared, seems like the best 'Fucking' option, then 'Fucking' ignorance.

You noticed, the 'F' Fucking word, was just used. Let us see, what eventuates, while I am typing this, to you.

See, it is already started. Power of words transmitting its way to you.

A surge, of energy takes over, and before I knew it, I was swearing, like a trooper.

Ask the 'Alien entity. Those, that know me, know, I do not usually swear, and if I have too, it changes, my energy level, and my mind, goes into the other world, of the alien world entity .

Especially lately, when I started, to give in to, the 'swear fucking words. Saying 'Bloody this, and bloody that', a lot, is not, the same thing.

As I have said it, that many times, in conversations.

It has, no effect, on the 'Alien entity'. They will test you, to generate, whatever energy, they can receive, from you. So far, I discovered, only, some words do!

Alien entity, thrives on 'F' and 'B' words, as in Fucking, Bitch, Bastard' etc.

I wrote a short story, with swear words, to see what happens, when the 'Alien entity', realises, I am typing the story.

A friend gave me the 'Right Title to use'. It surprised me of what I ended writing because of the title.

'The Alien entity' willingly gave me, whatever thoughts, that came to mind, to write the book, with humour, and swear words!

Remember, we are, who we are, with the Invisible 'Alien Entity' with us!

The 'Alien entity' or 'Spirit 'entity', is much linked together, as one source.   Imagine, looking at a 'skeleton'.

The 'Alien entity', becomes invisible, and those, who make an appearance, appear to have 'big eyes', like the eyes of a skull.

The skull eyes, are big and empty, While the 'Alien eyes are big and small,  and glow in the dark'.

Some people, may have sighted one, but it would have vanished, quickly.  Then, you have not much, to go on.

That is how, they want it, to be.

Do not, entertain them, or they will, never leave.

You will, do it anyway, because they will fuck, with your brains.  That is what they do.  You have just been told. Right here, right now, as you are reading this.

They fuck,  with your brains, and they make you, say fucking words, that give, them power.  You become, their servant. You work, for 'The Alien entity'.

You are working for them, and not being paid.  Get the picture? You play the Slot/Poker Machines, because they use your brains, without your consent.

You are hypnotised, by 'The Alien entity', to do exactly that. Your mind, is in another world, the world of 'The Alien entity'.

You, do not realise it, until afterwards, when the shock, of losing money, and not, being able, to stop, becomes apparent, to you.

You are under attack of 'The Alien entity', because, they will, not let, your mind go.  Do you see the picture, now?

The only time, you walk away, is when, you have no more money, and then, you realise, something, made you not able, to walk away.  If only, you could tell, it was, 'The Alien entity'.

It was thriving, on the power, you are giving, the 'Alien entity'.  Imagine, the hold, it had over your mind.  It was fucking with your brains, and had you, under its control.

Imagine, what else, it can do, to your relationships, and jobs, etc.  That is how powerful, this 'Alien entity' is.

Your idea, of time, to escape, from your hard day, or emotional stress, by going, to places and such venues wherever the, gambling is.

You meet people there, and you do not realise, their mind is under the control, of 'The Alien entity'.

Not everyone is, but you are attracted, and in fact, magnetically, pulled towards, the people, on the slot/poker machines, or games tables, etc.

There is no way, in the world, that you suspected, 'the Alien entity presence'.  You go in there, to relax.

Before you know it, your mind becomes, lured to playing, the Poker Machine, or other gambling etc.

Some of you think, of it as, a 'Demonic Possession'.  Yeah right?

Something takes over your brain, and you surrender to it, because, you are under, a trance hypnotic, state of mind.

Well, same foking thing as saying 'the Alien Entity' is foking with your brain, right now.  Isn't it?

You see the 'Demon Devil' as the demonic substitute. Alternatively, whatever took over, your mind?

Then somehow, it gave your mind back to you.  It is all a fucking game, right.

Yes, your relationship too, it became, a game of chance.

Just like the Poker machine, became a game, of chance.

The idea, of winning big money, in any lottery, is a game of chance, might also be, fucking with your brain, one might say.

(The reason I am using, the 'F' words), is because, it is giving, them power, to continue telling me, what needs, to be said, and you know, you have to think, like one, to know them!

When, they are, inside your mind, the (Alien entity) connects, to the Spirit form, of those, that once lived, and continue living, through the 'Alien entity'.

You do not understand why, you think, you are going about, doing whatever, in your life, some serious, and some fun.

The 'Alien entity', makes you think, it is your idea, & some believe, it's, the Demonic Devil, and not, the 'Alien entity'.

Because, they believe that more, as it states, to them, in the Bible.

But in fact, whatever causes, 'Alienation' as a result, comes from the word, 'Alien, and Entity' tags, with it)!  Get the picture, of what, I am saying?

As for money!  They do not understand, the meaning of money.  Sometimes, you spend, as if you are, a Millionaire, but you do not, have much money, at all.

You know, you cannot afford to lose money, but somehow, you do.  Right?

Your mind, becomes, taken away, by something.  Right? You are not, being you, at that time!

You can be sure, that your brains, have been invaded by, the 'Alien entity'!  You are so clever, very talented, and yet, you are distracted, and did not realise it, until afterwards.

The 'Alien entity', borrowed your mind.  Yes, they fucked around, with your brains, and then, when finished, gave it back to you.

You then, regain your natural self, for a while, until they, come back again!

As for 'Relationships', you cannot afford to lose, a good relationship either, can you?

You had no idea, it was the interference, from the 'Alien entity', that got into, someone brains, and played one person, against the other!

They only understand one thing, and the thing is, gaining your fucking brain, to access power, of domination over human earthlings, on our Planet Earth!

That is just an example.  Too many examples to list. Relationships, is another example.

If you let them control you, they will take over, your mind! With Business too, they will learn, from you.

When they are finished, they will use your brain, against another person, to 'Alienate your association, with the other!  ('Hence, the term I used, 'Alienate, and the meaning behind, ''Alien entity')

That is how 'the Alien source' gets close to you and the other person.  Think about it.

The 'Alien way, of fucking with you, by first, getting to fuck with your brains, and the rest, will be history.

As they, gained access, to you, and those you exchange, eye contact, and words with, etc.

When things start to go wrong.  Ask yourself, why?  If you blame it on fate, destiny, evil curses, jinx, voodoo, spells, rituals, etc.

You should think who was behind it all.

Off Course, it had to be 'An Entity', that got, into the brain, of the people, who are, doing it all.

If the 'Alien entity' did not fuck, with their brains, they would not, have tried, any spells, rituals, curses, hexes, etc.

Humans do, because, of the 'Alien entity'.  That world, can only exist, because, the human race, exists.

One, feeds off, the other.  Alternatively, the World, would end, through a so-called, 'Hungry Strike'.

In other words, if you do not feed, or be fed, how can life remain?

Energy, is the source, and whatever, type of energy, is being used, 'Aliens, will use it well, to their own, advantage'.

Just, like Humans do.  Our Brains, are connected, to the 'Alien Life force'!

Nothing works, on its own, unless 'the brain of the person' starts, to plan it, or begins it.  The brain notices many, feelings, thoughts, energies etc.  The 'Alien entity', knows it.

Let us just say, my books, have all been read, by 'The Alien entity'.  After all, the 'Invisible source, is what came through, to connect, and make them, come about!

It is, not just about, 'Adam and Eve, in the so-called Garden of Eden, on Earth. Although, to each, their own beliefs.

I would like, to describe it, as about, Aliens and Human Earthling, in the Garden of Utopia.  Perhaps, that is the best way, I can describe it.

Nirvana, is the stop over, from the transition, from one world, to another.  Birth is the beginning, and death is the rebirth, which is connecting, to the 'Alien World', before, you are reborn.

Some of us, are growing older, but are feeling like, we are still young.  The 'Alien entity', has already, connected to you.

How much power, you give 'the Alien entity, and its source', will be, up to you.

Perhaps, that is why, some people go sooner, than others go, to the other world, and begin, their transition, to the 'Alien world'.

Alien abduction, of planes etc. has become something, worth discussing.

Unfortunately, they are invisible, and this becomes, a story without facts.  They require facts, as usual, to be believable.

The point, of it all is, the less you discover, about the 'Alien life force', the better, they will be, in keeping, their power source, under their control.

In addition, since they are linked, to earthlings, from the beginning of time, you would hate, to think, what would happen, if 'the Alien entity' came out, of the closet, and became, visible to everyone.

It could cause, an outbreak of war, perhaps earth, would be destroyed, in the process.  Therefore, its best, left alone.

You cannot, fight them, and it is impossible, to fight something, that you cannot, have control over, due to being invisible.

Yes, they are superior in that way.  They also know we have what they need too.  In addition, we look superior to them.

Someone once told you 'choose your words carefully'. Remember, we have been told that at times. Tell me which words might help the situation you are in?

Like someone, said to you, 'I Love You', and yet they hurt you. Let us see, if that came, from the 'Alien Source'.

Why hurt someone? Are you that desperate, to feed off, the hurt, of another? Is that what humans do? Are earthlings, created to hurt, each other?

It does not, make sense, that a human body, wants to hurt another human. Animals do, for food, and to defend themselves, from other animals.

However, Human brains are usually, innocent, when born. Right?

OK, but something fucking got into their brains, and made them act, not from, a human behaviour.

The Beast, or wild animals, only know, to fight for survival. The 'Alien' also is, the same. Get the picture.

They are afraid, of being destroyed. Earthlings are a threat, to the 'Alien world'. That is why, humans behave the way, they do, because of the 'Alien entity' that fucks, with the human brain.

The takeover, of Planet Earth, is already in place. Perhaps, not like a war, as you might imagine, it to be. More like, the smarter you are, at University, and the power goes, to you.

Such, is the idea, of the 'Alien world'. They can only use, your brains, to gain access, to your knowledge.

Yes, they are smarter, only because, we did not know, they had been, learning from earthlings, all along, from the beginning of time.

If they can, upset you, they will.  This is due, to turning on, your power source, and that is, what they want, from you. Your mind, becomes them, and their mind, becomes yours.

'A fair exchange'.  Some might say, when you're fucking stoned, on weed.

The less, you question, the idea, of an 'Alien entity, being present', its much kinder done, while you are stoned, on weed.  As some people, might say!

Once again, that would only be, a quick easy access, to your brain, as the 'Alien' is fucking with it, without any trouble! ☺

Saying the word Bitch' or 'Bastard', makes, the 'Alien, stand at attention. ☺

You have joined the 'Elite', in the 'Alien school do knowledge'.  Any word that makes your body come to an 'alert stage', at 'attention stage', makes your energy power source connect to some outlet that needs to be charged.

Yes, 'Aliens are experts' of what, gives off power, and what depletes, power.  The 'Alien world' lives off, 'human power source, and animal power source'.

'The Alien entity', is foking with your brains, because, that is how, they integrate, with human earthlings.  They feed on knowledge.

In some way, I wish, I did get, a 'Harvard Degree' of some kind, to make the 'Aliens' happy!

However, it was not, to be, and they knew, I could sense, they are present, and they wised up, to the fact, off power struggles.

They do not want, to fight over power, and if you, understand that, you will understand, the meaning of, 'they just want, to take it'.  Easy take over!  Get the picture?

It is easy, when you are feeling vulnerable, for them to 'Take over'.  Because, they do not like, power struggles, and least resistance, is more of a power surge, to the Alien entity!

For example, when a dog is wounded, they are likely to bite attack etc.  They are, at their most, vulnerable state.

They sense, the 'Alien entity' present, and would do whatever they can to stop the 'Alien entity' getting to them!

The problem is, 'The Alien entity' will use a human brain, too, and fuck with their brains, making them, do, and act, not in a human way.  The dog, will attack, the human, because, it is sensing, it is under attack, from the 'Alien entity'!

Now, tell me, why they call a dog a 'Bytch'?  Yes, I know, it is the name, of a dog.  However, It is the 'word, that carries a sound, when said, that carries, a power source, of energy to the 'Alien entity'!  Keep that in mind.  Some words, are powerful.

You see what I mean.  Whenever they hear, powerful vibrating, resonating words, it carries power, to which then, the Alien entity, will plug into, its source.  (Which becomes, the Earthling).  Because they carry, the source, and feed it, to the Alien entity.  Get the picture now?

Earthlings are their source of power!  Because Earthling is capable, of much knowledge, and displaying, their knowledge, makes the 'Alien', want to join, the 'Earthling, & Alien Talent Quest'!

Obviously, too much talent, does go to their heads.  Like at school, when a show off student, becomes like, a smarty ass, putting their hand up, to answer, every question possible!

No doubt, the 'Alien entity' is watching, and ready to use their brains, so they can learn, from all knowledge, that the student, gives them.

Remember, the more eager you are, to advance in your world, eventually, you will notice, most advancement, comes at a price.  Whatever job, you get into.

The reason, we do, talk about 'Alien beings', very much, is because, it can cause 'panic' on Earth.  We do not, want that.

There is nothing, to panic about, with 'Aliens taking over, planet Earth'.  (Though that remark, would have you, cracking up laughing, or talking about it, like crazy)

Those of you who welcome 'The Alien entity', do so while stoned on your weed or take precautions to be friendly with them, or go against at your own risk.

Just remember, they are learning, from Earthlings.  If you are angry, they will feed, on that energy.

If you are totally, stoned out of your mind, on good weed, and it smells like, the green, green, grass of an Aliens Home, they will accept, your talent, as favourable.

You are most likely, wondering why, 'An Alien entity' prefers, to see you accept them, instead of, going against them.

You become easy to observe, as they become 'Alien Pot Heads'.  They catch your bad habits, and it soon becomes their bad habits.

You have all seen what an 'Alien being' looks like in a Movie.  Haven't you?

They look even better, when you have had a few drinks of Vodka, too!

Seriously, though, their identity, can change.  Which might, baffle those, who have captured them, and are keeping them, for safekeeping?

Meanwhile, as they study these 'Aliens', Earthlings are in turn, being studied, and their brain, being takeover, by them.

Do not just blame, your 'attitude' on the 'Full Moon effect'. That generally, is for the Wolves, to howl at, and connect to its, Moon powerful source.

Having said that, 'Alien beings stay in their invisible disguise, and only use their 'Entity' to connect.

Meanwhile, Humans, love the moon, and because of this, 'The Alien entity', knows very well, that you must carry some type, of powerful energy, of which, they love to absorb, from the brain, of an Earthling.

Making peace, with your 'Alien' is the first step, to acceptance.  Telling them, you come in peace, will also make them, and want to tell you, the same likewise.

Remember, whatever you do, which causes them, to feel under threat, will only make matters worse, and not better. Just because, they learning, from Earthlings.

If you tell them, and make them, feel that you are, at war, with them, it will only become, a 'U.F.O battleground, on Earth.

We, do not, want that, do we?  Keep calm, and send happy thoughts, to your 'Alien entity'. ☺

In case, you feel overwhelmed, by the 'Alien entity', you will notice, you cannot control, your words, or your actions.

 It just means, there is an overload, of too much power surge, etc.

When you notice that, sit and listen to music that calms you, and or drink or eat something.

Reason being is, it requires a way, of unplugging yourself, from the 'Alien entity, outlet'.

 Just like, you plug something electrical, into the power point.

You unplug it, when you do not need, the power from it. Right?   It applies to the Human Earthling, energy power source.

If you, are wondering, why am I able to write, about it, without, the 'Alien entity', being upset, with me.  Well, they are upset, that I can link, into both worlds, & write about it.

They didn't expect, that type of communication.  And that, I was able, to control it.  Once you, become linked, to their Alien entity world, they usually then, control you.

They didn't expect me, to have the power, to detach from their control, & continue what I do, my way.

I can feel the sudden surge, of power, taking over, and making me, very restless.

However, I have mastered, the control of it, to an extent. Though, not quiet, all of it.  They know, I need money.

They know, you need money, but they do not know, the meaning, of money.  They know, you are thinking of it, because, it is your brains, they are, hitching a ride on.

They know, you want a good job, or any job.  They know also, that you have No Job, and not able, to earn money, because you think, about money.

They will play on our weakness to make us human earthlings restless enough to be tempted into many things, and 'Gambling', is just one of them concerning money!

I bet they also love, to enter the mind, of those, who seek power, in the Government & other powerful roles.

And 'role play', the 'alien entity', does very well.

They know, you want that role, or job, and they will hitch, a ride, to gain access, into your brain, to gain power, of knowledge, from it.  The 'Alien entity' is so cunning, and yet so connected, to humans, that they, can influence, the human race!

Yes, 'the Alien entity' will do that, quite easy, to those who are vulnerable.  They will seek out, your weakness, and use it against you.  Remember that!

Whatever your weakness is, they will use it against you!

That is 'The Alien way'.  Aliens have control, over your mind, to an extent, and when you realise it, you stop giving, your power, over to them.

However, it is not always, easy to do!

Sometimes, people would call it, 'Psychic Attack', and not 'Alien entity'.  In the past, I would have agreed, to an extent of Psychic Mind, stealing interference.

However, it has to come, from somewhere, and that is why, I tend to think, 'It's the source, and the source, is the Alien entity'.

It needs, a source.  Doesn't it?  If you find out, what the source is, you have, the main culprit.

A human Earthling, can only use their mind, as best, they know how. In addition, if it is, being interfered with, it has to come, from a source, and the 'Alien entity', is what, the source is.

The best way is, when you suspect you are not being able to be yourself, stop, and do the opposite, to confuse the 'Alien source'.

You are in fact allowing them to learn from you, what they do not want to learn.  Get the picture?  It sounds funny too. Teaching them, a bad education! ☺

That teaches them also, this is what happens when they fuck with your brains!  They get the run around and no wiser than when they first fucked with your brains!

Remember, the twin effect.  You see a person, but you do not always see their invisible twin with them.  Do you?

The "Alien entity' will enter your mind without you knowing, and the people you are around.

They cannot communicate with you because they are of an 'Alien entity'.  However, they can use you, to gain access to learning from you and those around you!  Remember as in the 'Twin effect'.

One twin can read and feel what another twin is thinking or feeling, at times.  'The Alien entity' works on the same pattern of thought.

It links to your mind, and fucks with your brains, in order to access knowledge, for the 'Alien world'.  After all, they thrive, the only way, they know, how.

Likewise, Earthlings Humans, are much the same, learning and thriving, the best way, they know how!

Unfortunately, you cannot get rid of them, as they are part of the human earthling existence, connected to us, from the beginning of time!

Just a word of caution.  If you suspect, your brains are being fucked with, by an 'Alien entity', do not bother entertaining them, as they are likely to crash your party!

In addition, No Doubt any political party for that matter!

We are all human earthlings and we make mistakes, and that is why they love seeing us make mistakes.

This gives them, more power to use coming from us & then used against us, Human Earthlings, on Planet earth!

A and for the empty blank pages for you to write your thought on ☺ Also wild Photography I did, for you to be inspired with!

Author Jacqueline Howard


Please Note:  No Names in this Book are of Real, Living Human Earthlings.

All My Books are Purely for Entertainment Purposes.

**My Books & Movie Scripts are as follows.**

www.amamzon.com/author/funbooksjacquelinehoward


**DETANRACNI (Movie script Book)**

**V for Vodka (Movie Script Book)**

**Love & Destruction (Trilogy) Movie script Books 1/ Escape from Eternity 2/Angels World of The Gods 3/Loves A Killer**

**Wolf Bloodline (Trilogy) 1/Wolf Bloodline 2/Revenge of Wolf Bloodline 3/The Dark Lord & The Curse**

**Bella On Playboy**

**Bambe & Toyboy**

**Skeletons R Us**

**Big Ted**

**Nirvana In The Spirit Kurt Cobain**

**Twin Flame For My Emily**

**On The Buses**

**The Screw**

**Kiss My Mantra**

**Like Aliens Hitching A Ride On Human Brains**

**You Are My Kind Of Alien**

**Song Lyrics**

**A Book of Lyrics**

**Teen Wolverine**

**The Directors Cut**

**Black Moon Karma**

**Philosophy Made Simple**

**Star Signs For Lovers**

**Dating Rulez**

**Author Jacqueline Howard**

**Email : Lovechiald@hotmail.com**

**Donations to:  PayPal.Me/lovechilds**

30

This Page Is a Special Thanks to All Those In (The Spirit World & The Alien Entity) that came through in the making of this Book.

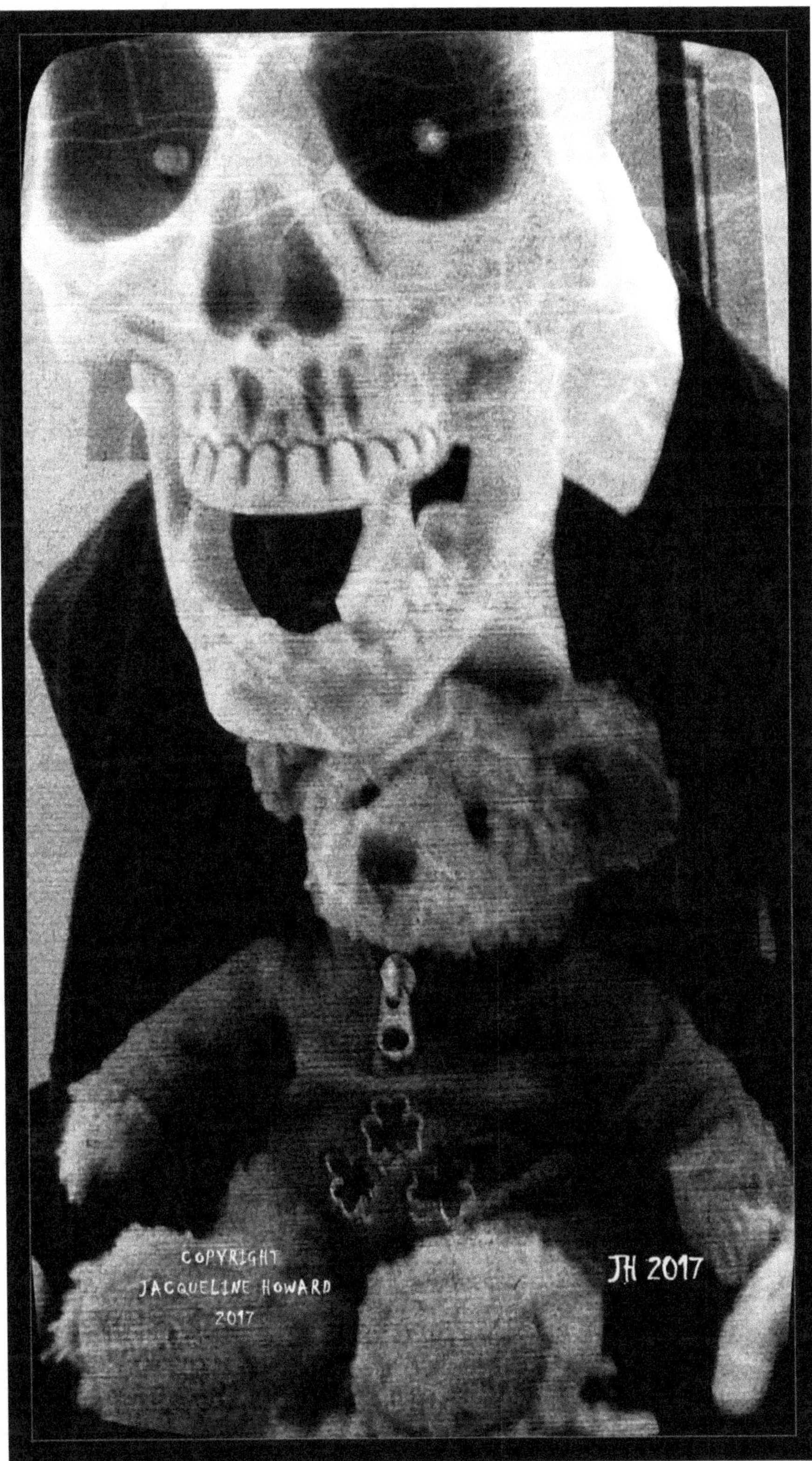

COPYRIGHT
JACQUELINE HOWARD
2017

JH 2017

©Jacqueline Howard 2012 www.jackie666.blog.com  http://www.amazon.com/dp/B005ZS2TR4

© Jacqueline Howard 2011
Artist Jacqueline Howard   www.jackie666.blog.com
Jackie HOWARD

WWW.LOVECHILD.BLOGSPOT.COM BY JACQUELINE HOWARD 2016

©copyright J Howard 2013  Author & Photographer J Howard www.jackie666.blog.com

42

No
Money

No
Honey
Author & Photographer J Honard 2017
www.lovechiald.blogspot.com

44

**Notes:**

**This Page Is for the Readers who may wish to write In.**

©2015 copyright Jacqueline Howard

God Helps Those
Who Help
Themself
To
Everything
Jacqueline Howard 2017 Author & Photographer
www.lovechiald.blogspot.com
http://www.amazon.com/dp/B0075440PA  ©J Howard 2012

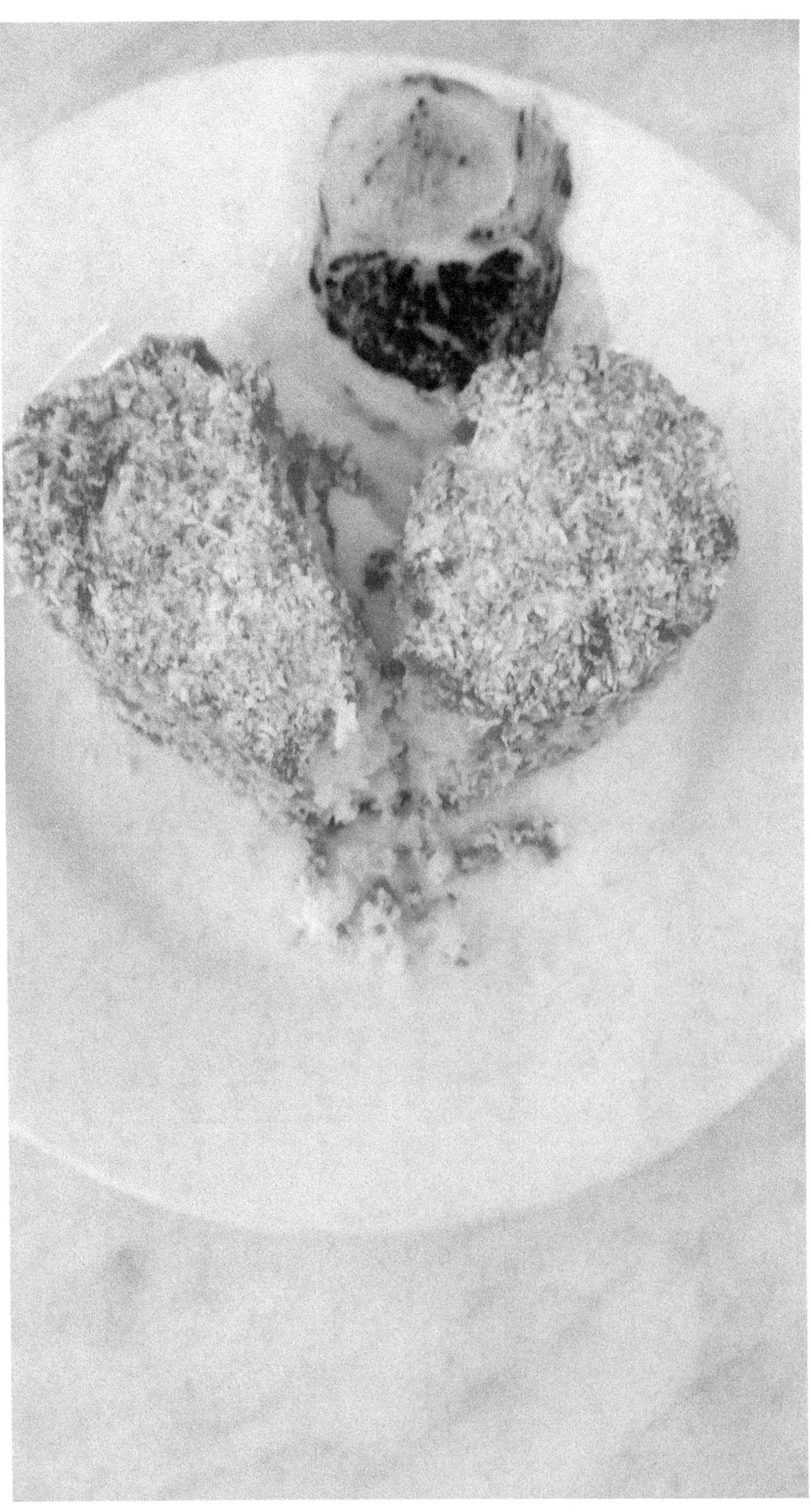

Author & Photographer © Jacqueline Howard 2012

OMG
ITS
YOU
Author & Photographer J Howard 2017
www.lovechiald.blogspot.com

BIG
TED
A LOTCOA
Author & Photography Jacqueline Howard 2017 www.lovechiald.blogspot.com

Author & Photography
By Jacqueline Howard 2017

13/01/2017

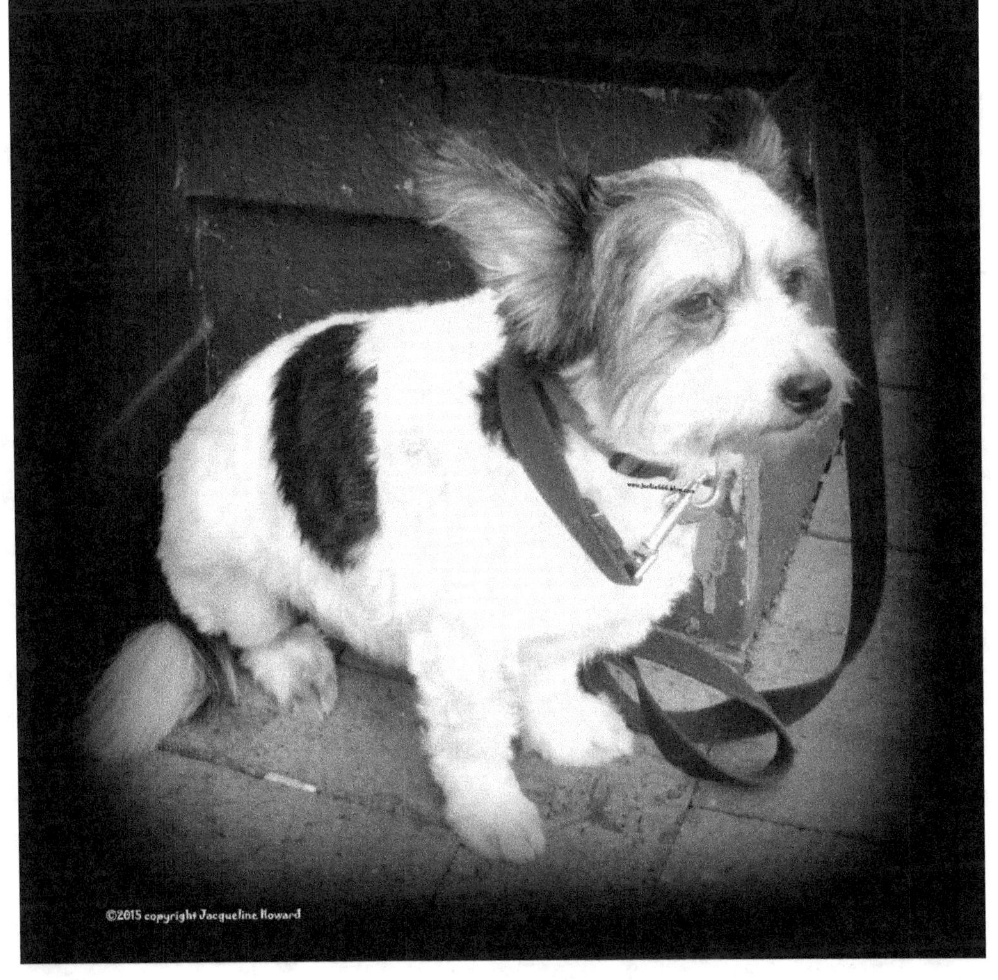
©2015 copyright Jacqueline Howard

22/01/2017

God Helps Those
Who Help
Themself
To
Everything
Jacqueline Howard 2017 Author & Photographer
www.lovechiald.blogspot.com
http://www.amazon.com/dp/B0075440PA  ©J Howard 2012

2011/05/20

Author & Photographer  © Jacqueline Howard 2012

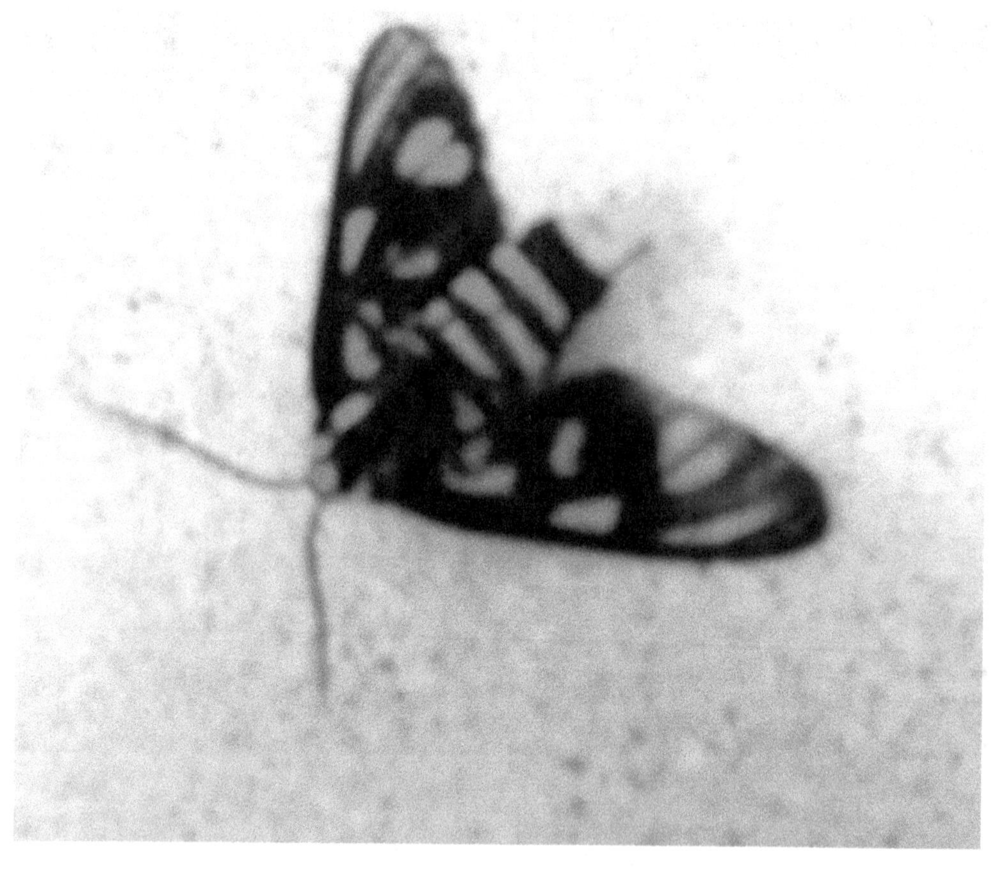

©copyright Jacqueline Howard 2013  July Moon 2013 Sydney Australia  www.jackie666.blog.com

66

©copyright J Howard 2013  Author & Photographer J Howard www.jackie666.blog.com

God Helps Those
Who Help
Themself
To
Everything
Jacqueline Howard 2017 Author & Photographer
www.lovechiald.blogspot.com
http://www.amazon.com/dp/B0075440PA  ©J Howard 2012

©copyright J Howard 2013  Author & Photographer J Howard www.jackie666.blog.com

Author & Photography
By Jacqueline Howard 2017

2011/05/20

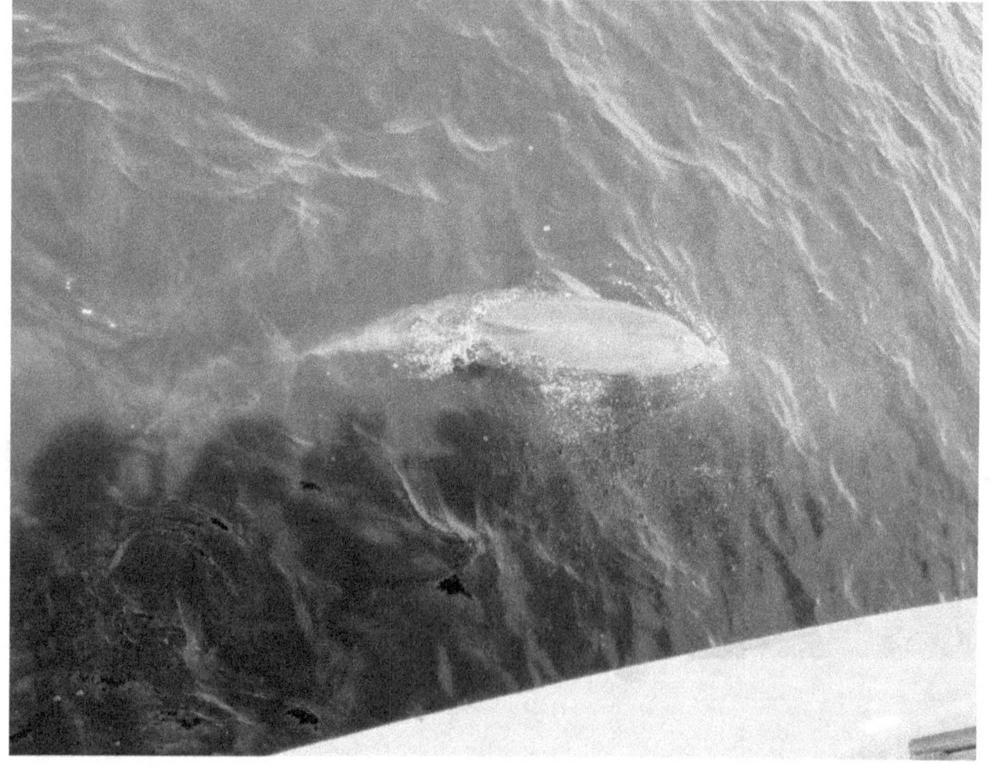

©2015 copyright Jacqueline Howard

God Helps Those
Who Help
Themself
To
Everything
Jacqueline Howard 2017 Author & Photographer
www.lovechiald.blogspot.com
http://www.amazon.com/dp/B0075440PA  ©J Howard 2012

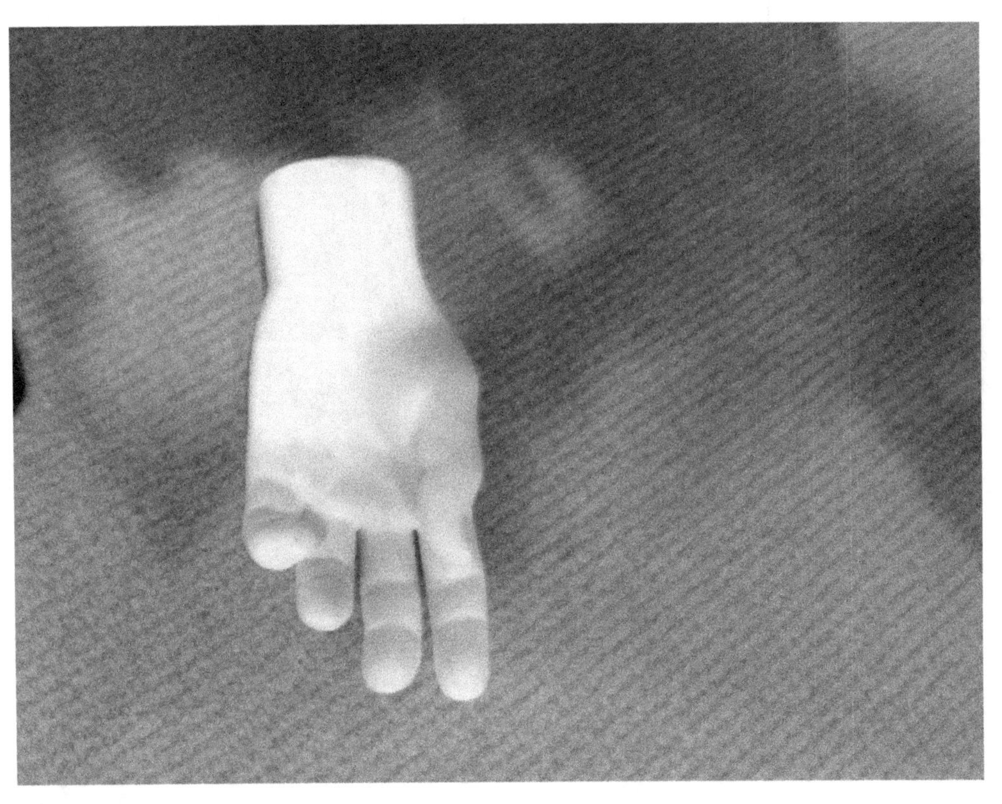

KING OF KONG
SAYS...

GIVE A LITTLE
SHIT

ITS BETTER
OUT
THAN IN

Author & Photographer Jacqueline Howard
WWW.LOVECHIALD.BLOGSPOT.COM

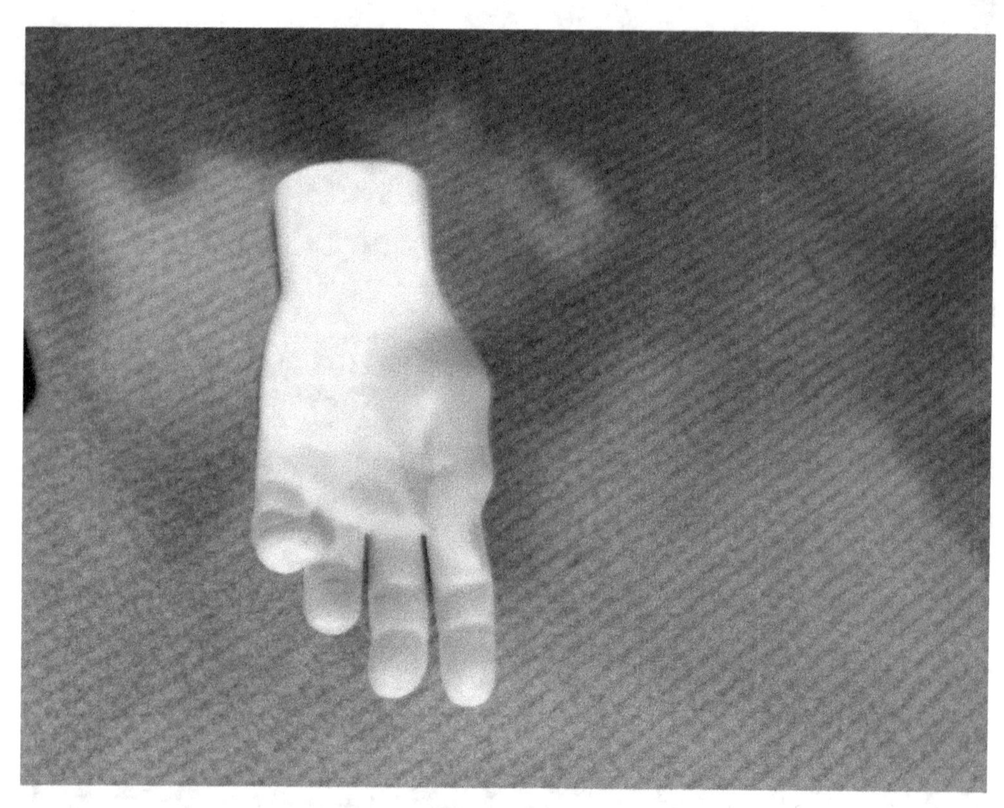

©copyright J Howard 2013  Author & Photographer J Howard www.jackie666.blog.com

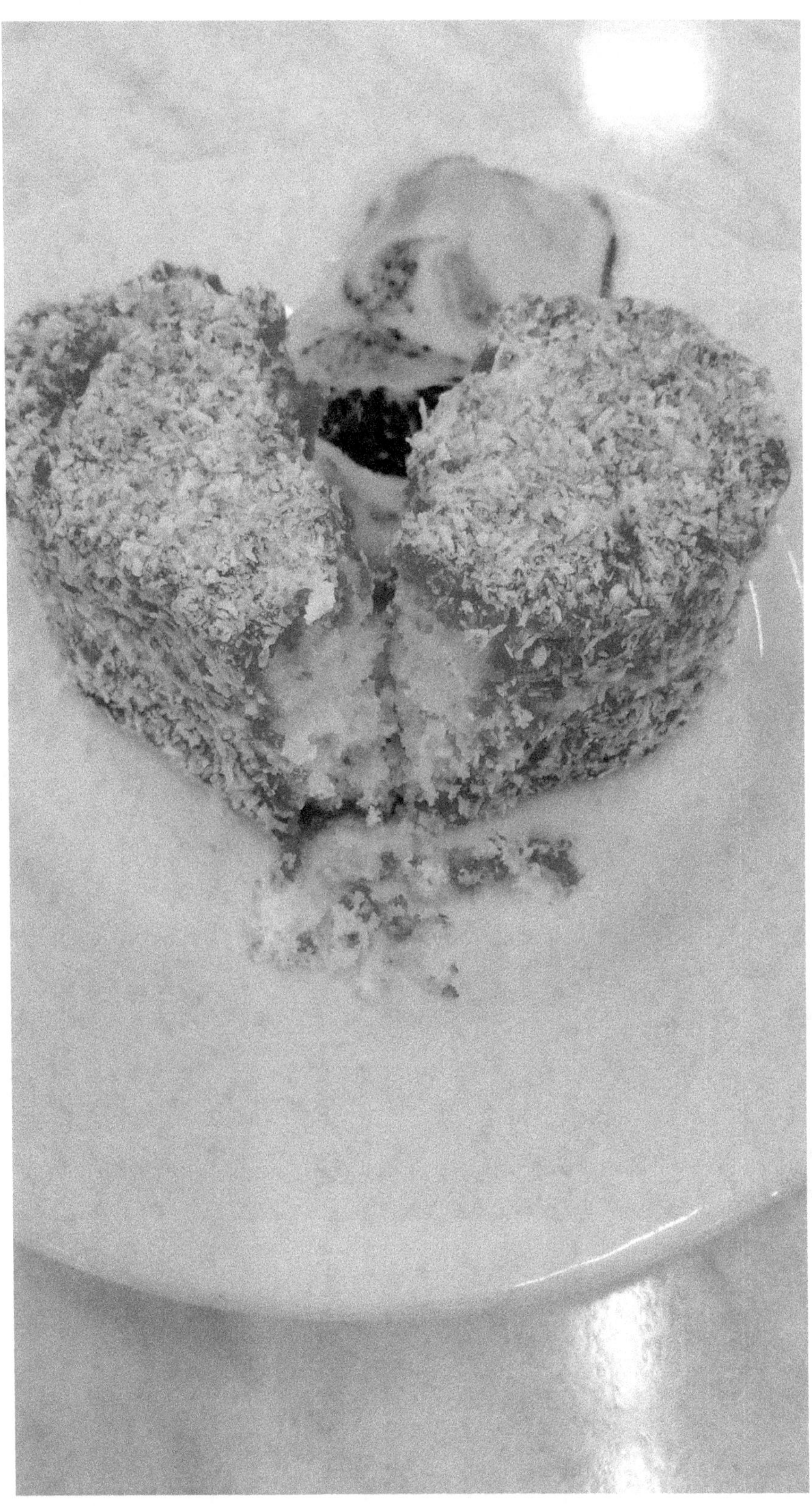

©2015 copyright Jacqueline Howard

God Helps Those
Who Help
Themself
To
Everything
Jacqueline Howard 2017 Author & Photographer
www.lovechild.blogspot.com
http://www.amazon.com/dp/B0075440PA  ©J Howard 2012

BIG TED
A LOTOA
Author & Photography Jacqueline Howard 2017 www.lovechiald.blogspot.com

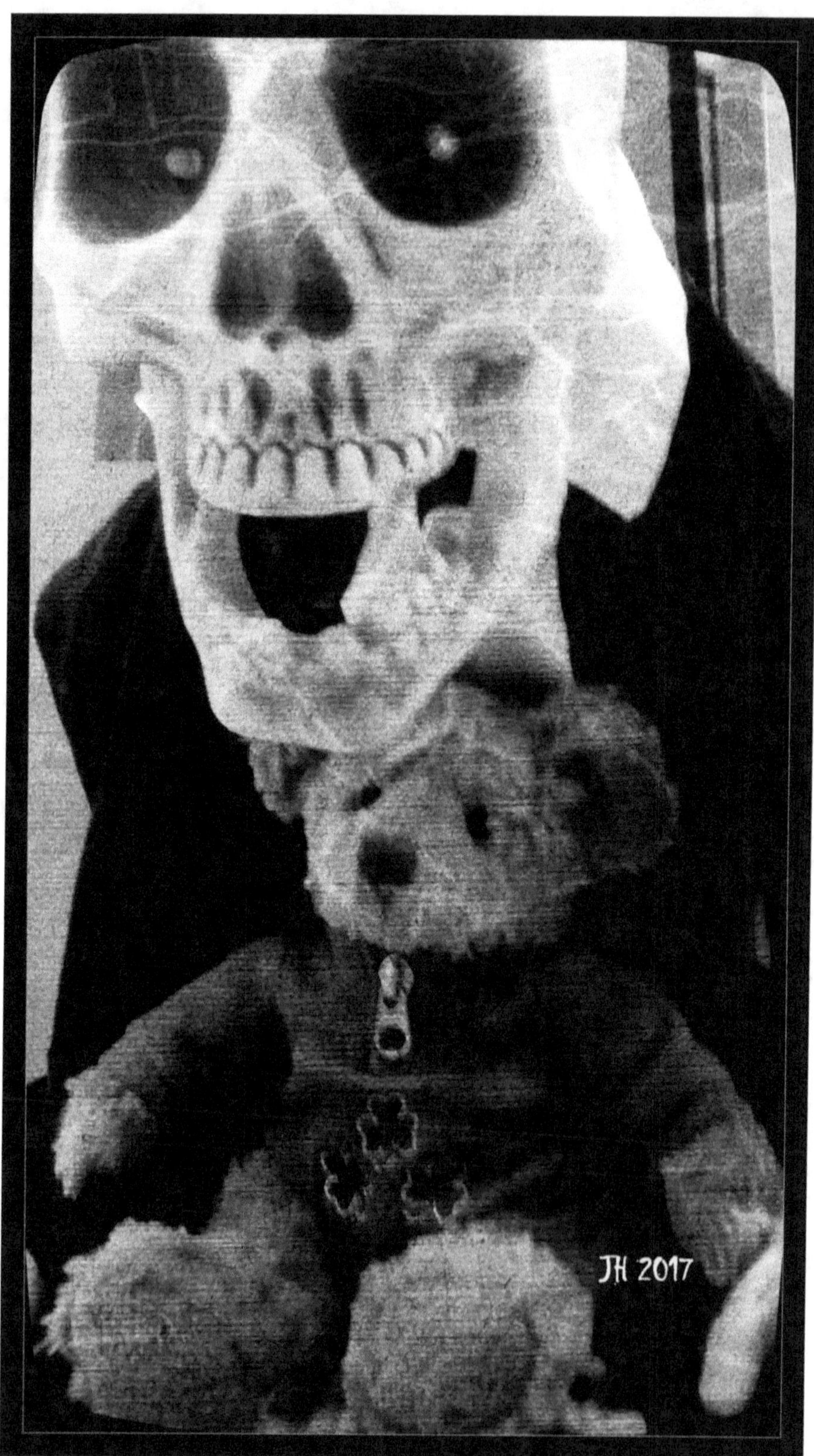
JH 2017

www.supernaturalport.blogspot.com

God Helps Those
Who Help
Themself
To
Everything
Jacqueline Howard 2017 Author & Photographer
www.lovechiald.blogspot.com
http://www.amazon.com/dp/B0075440PA  ©J Howard 2012

Author & Photo by J Howard 2017
www.lovechiald.blogspot.com

God Helps Those
Who Help
Themself
To
Everything
Jacqueline Howard 2017 Author & Photographer
www.lovechiald.blogspot.com
http://www.amazon.com/dp/B0075440PA  ©J Howard 2012

©copyright J Howard 2013  Author & Photographer J Howard www.jackie666.blog.com

KING OF KONG
SAYS...
WATCH THE HAND
DUMMY

THE HAND
YOU DIDNT SEE
IS YOUR
GOOD AND BAD
KARMA

Author & Photographer Jacqueline Howard
WWW.LOVECHIALD.BLOGSPOT.COM

God Helps Those
Who Help
Themself
To
Everything
Jacqueline Howard 2017 Author& Photographer
www.lovechiald.blogspot.com
http://www.amazon.com/dp/B0075440PA  ©J Howard 2012

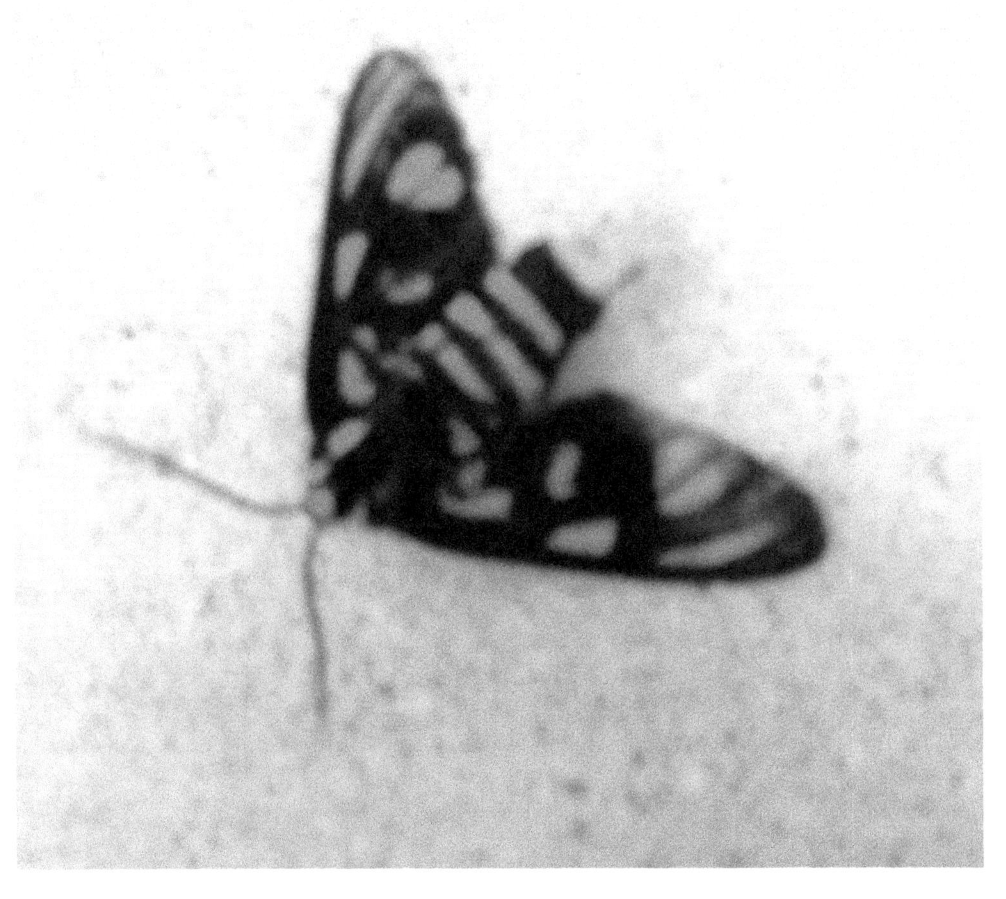

©copyright J Howard 2013  Author & Photographer J Howard www.jackie666.blog.com

God Helps Those
Who Help
Themself
To
Everything
Jacqueline Howard 2017 Author& Photographer
www.lovechiald.blogspot.com
http://www.amazon.com/dp/B0075440PA  ©J Howard 2012

22/01/2017

LOVE
THE
ONE
THAT
GIVES
A
DAMN
bY j hOWARD 2017
LOVECHIALD.BLOGSPOT.COM

On FunNY FARM
NO IFS
JusT BuTTS
©copyright Jacqueline 2012
www.jackie666.blog.com

YAMAHA

Thankyou for tuning in to my Book Titled 'Like Aliens Hitching a Ride on Human Brains'.  Author J Howard 2018.

Photography J Howard 2018.

Thanks again for reading my book and wild uplifting creative photography.

You can also check all my other books and photography.  There is 'Ten Book' including Movie scripts, so far.  Browse through and see what you like.

Author Jacqueline Howard.

## Like Aliens Hitching a Ride on Human Brains

©J Howard 2018

Author Jacqueline Howard/Like Aliens Hitching a Ride on Human Brains©2018

Photography by Jacqueline Howard

www.amamzon.com/author/funbooksjacqueline

More than 32+ books & movie scripts.

Author & Photography
By Jacqueline Howard 2017

KING OF KONG
SAYS...

GIVE A LITTLE
SHIT

ITS BETTER
OUT
THAN IN

Author & Photographer Jacqueline Howard
WWW.LOVECHIALD.BLOGSPOT.COM

2011/05/20

©2015 copyright Jacqueline Howard

God Helps Those
Who Help
Themself
To
Everything
Jacqueline Howard 2017 Author & Photographer
www.lovechiald.blogspot.com
http://www.amazon.com/dp/B0075440PA  ©J Howard 2012

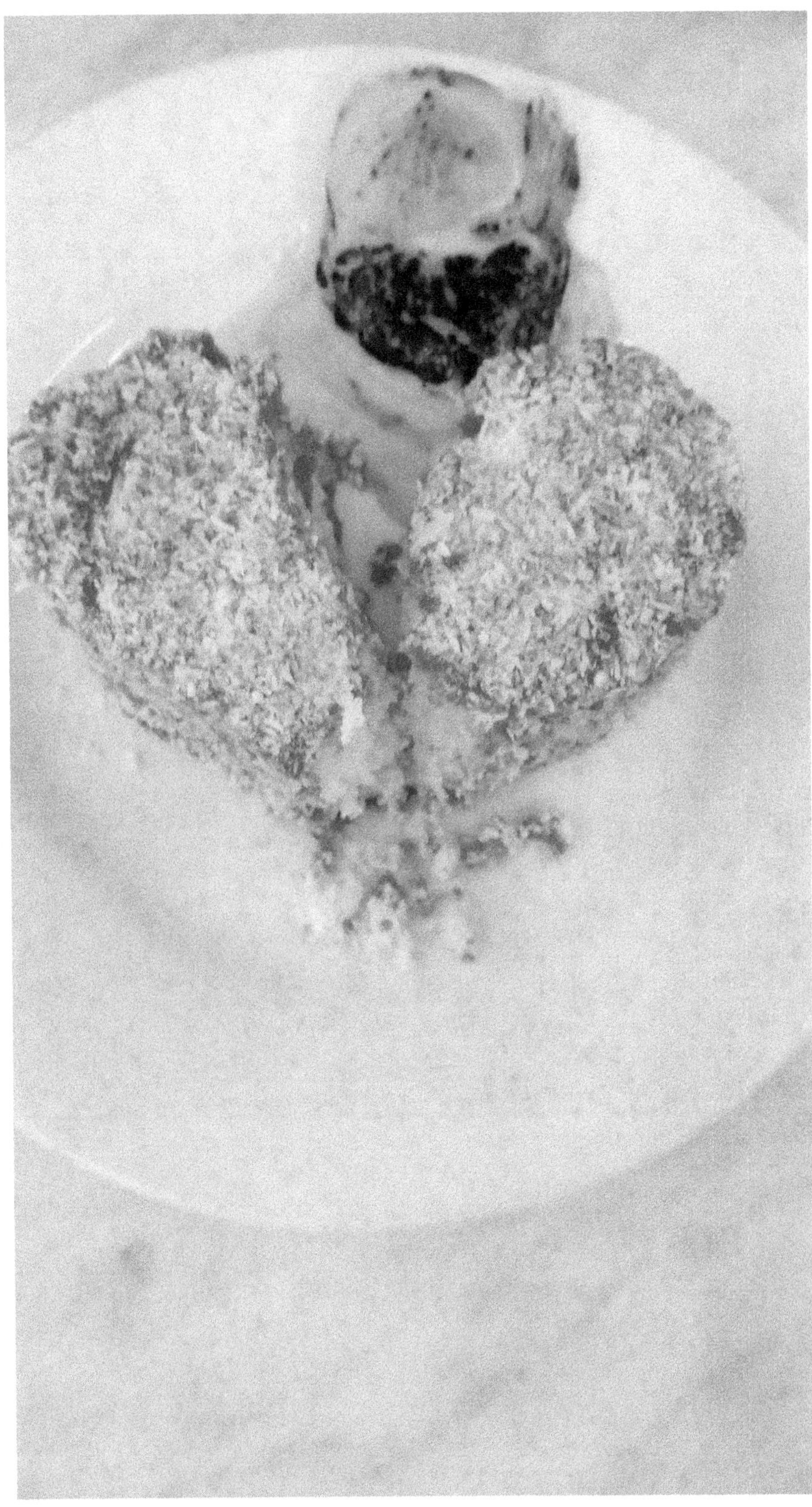

Author & Photographer  © Jacqueline Howard 2012

OMG
ITS
YOU
Author & Photographer J Honard 2017
www.lovechiald.blogspot.com

BIG
TED
A LOTOOA
Author & Photography Jacqueline Howard 2017 www.lovechiald.blogspot.com

Author & Photography
By Jacqueline Howard 2017

13/01/2017

©2015 copyright Jacqueline Howard

137

God Helps Those
Who Help
Themself
To
Everything
Jacqueline Howard 2017 Author & Photographer
www.lovechiald.blogspot.com
http://www.amazon.com/dp/B0075440PA  ©J Howard 2012

142

Author & Photographer © Jacqueline Howard 2012

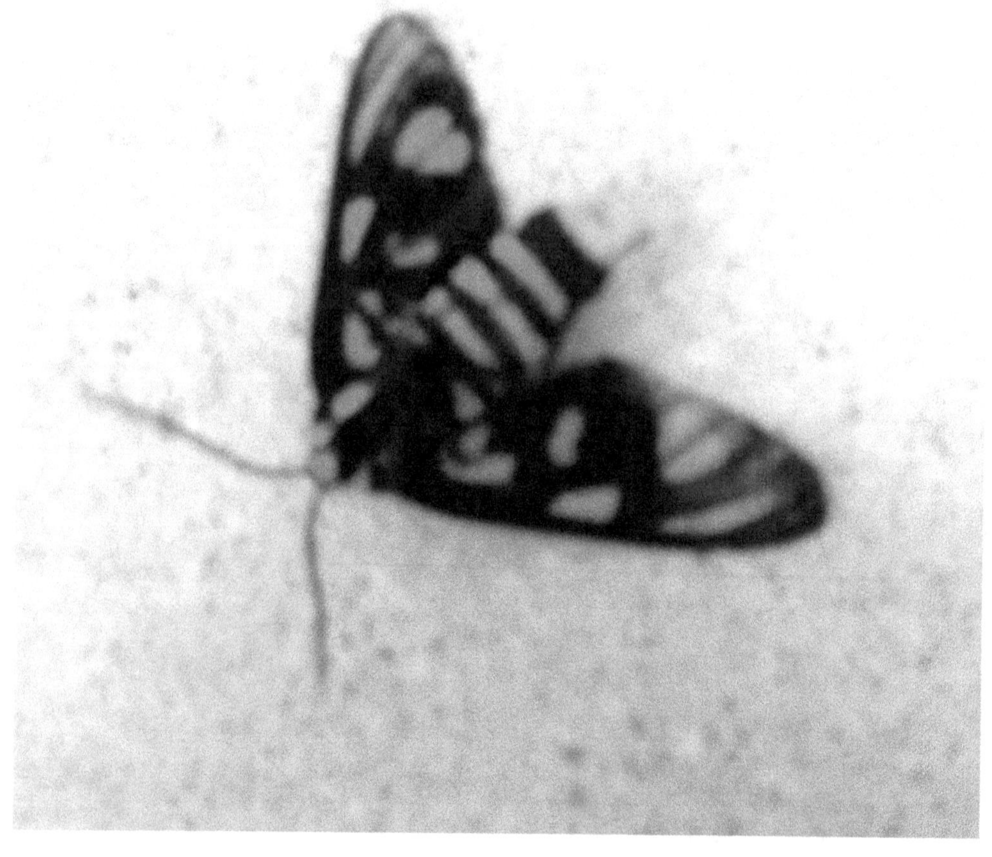

©copyright Jacqueline Howard 2013  July Moon 2013 Sydney Australia  www.jackie666.blog.com

148

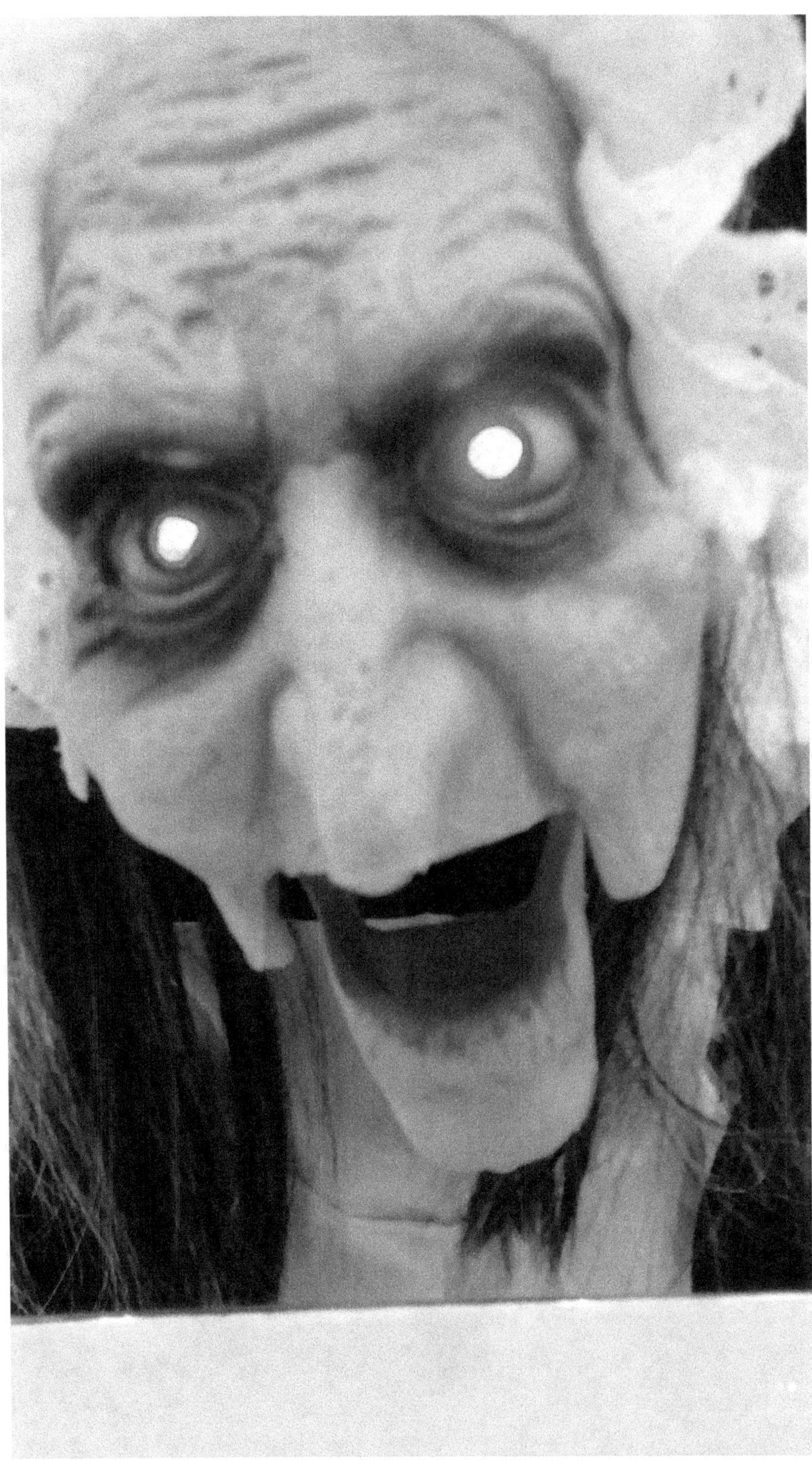

©copyright J Howard 2013  Author & Photographer J Howard www.jackie666.blog.com

WISHING POND HAS BEEN TOUCHED WITH
MYSTICAL MAGICAL POWERS BY ME
BURWOOD SYDNEY NSW AUSTRALIA 2017
WWW.LOVECHIALD.BLOGSPOT.COM

God Helps Those
Who Help
Themself
To
Everything
Jacqueline Howard 2017 Author & Photographer
www.lovechiald.blogspot.com
http://www.amazon.com/dp/B0075440PA  ©J Howard 2012

©copyright J Howard 2013  Author & Photographer J Howard www.jackie666.blog.com

Author & Photography
By Jacqueline Howard 2017

2011/05/20

©2015 copyright Jacqueline Howard

God Helps Those
Who Help
Themself
To
Everything
Jacqueline Howard 2017 Author & Photographer
www.lovechiald.blogspot.com
http://www.amazon.com/dp/B0075440PA  ©J Howard 2012

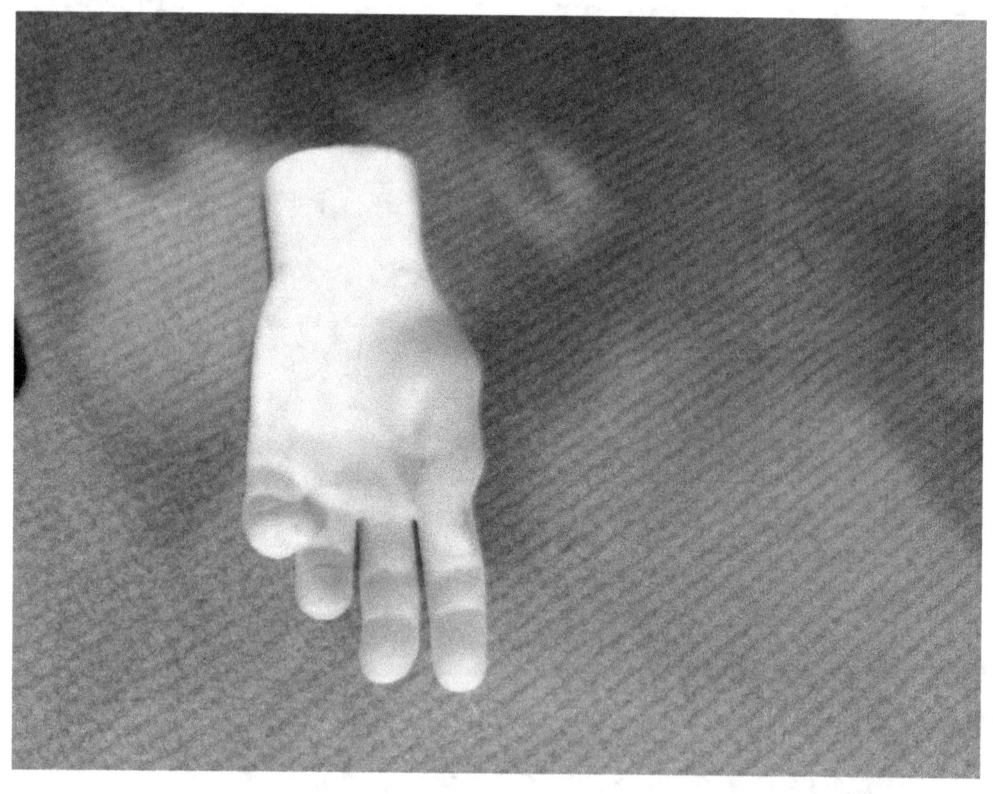

KING OF KONG
SAYS...

GIVE A LITTLE
SHIT

ITS BETTER
OUT
THAN IN

Author & Photographer Jacqueline Howard
WWW.LOVECHIALD.BLOGSPOT.COM

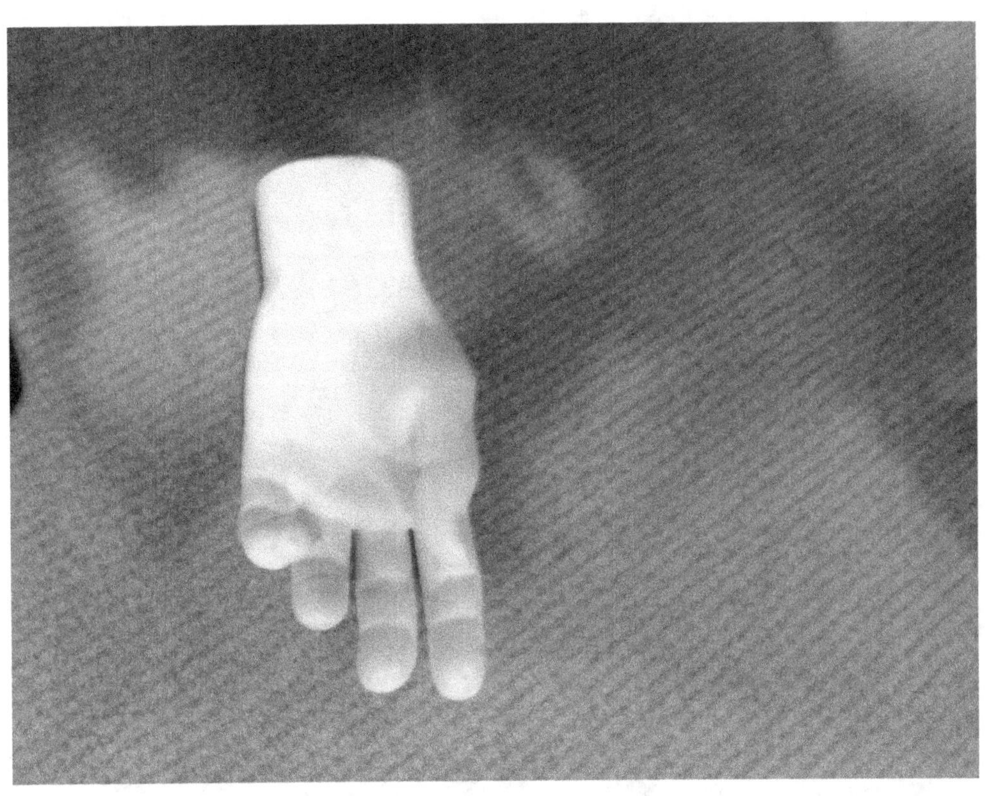

©copyright J Howard 2013  Author & Photographer J Howard www.jackie666.blog.com

©2015 copyright Jacqueline Howard

God Helps Those
Who Help
Themself
To
Everything
Jacqueline Howard 2017 Author & Photographer
www.lovechiald.blogspot.com
http://www.amazon.com/dp/B0075440PA  ©J Howard 2012

BIG
TED
A LOTOOF
Author & Photography Jacqueline Howard 2017 www.lovechiald.blogspot.com

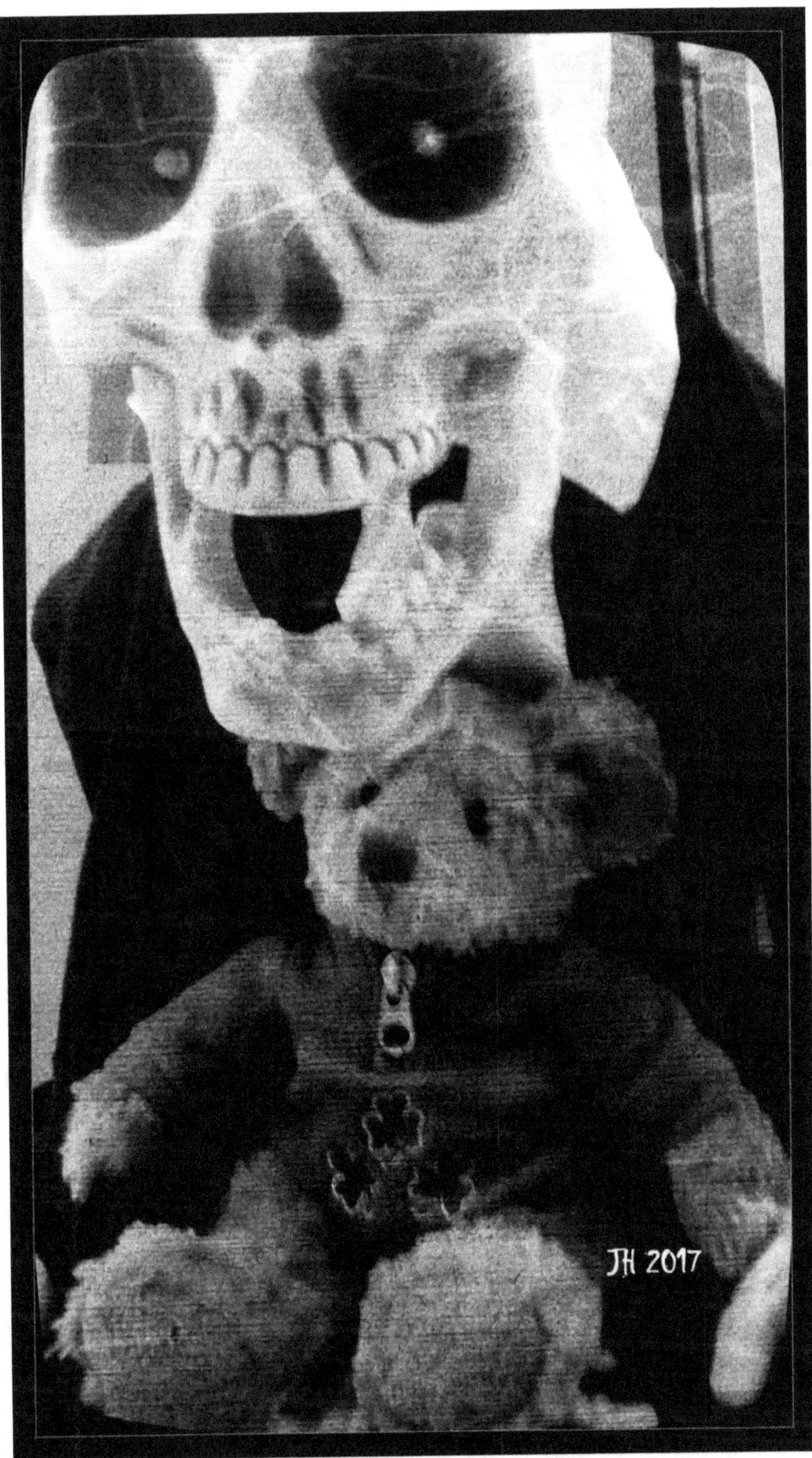
JH 2017

Author & Photographer © Jacqueline Howard 2012

God Helps Those
Who Help
Themself
To
Everything
Jacqueline Howard 2017 Author & Photographer
www.lovechiald.blogspot.com
http://www.amazon.com/dp/B0075440PA  ©J Howard 2012

180

Author & Photo by J Howard 2017
www.lovechiald.blogspot.com

God Helps Those
Who Help
Themself
To
Everything
Jacqueline Howard 2017 Author& Photographer
www.lovechiald.blogspot.com
http://www.amazon.com/dp/B0075440PA  ©J Howard 2012

©copyright J Howard 2013  Author & Photographer J Howard www.jackie666.blog.com

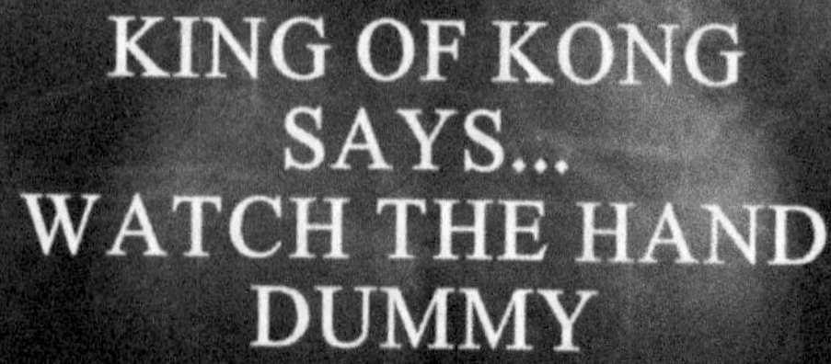


KING OF KONG
SAYS...
WATCH THE HAND
DUMMY

THE HAND
YOU DIDNT SEE
IS YOUR
GOOD AND BAD
KARMA

Author & Photographer Jacqueline Howard
WWW.LOVECHIALD.BLOGSPOT.COM

God Helps Those
Who Help
Themself
To
Everything
Jacqueline Howard 2017 Author& Photographer
www.lovechiald.blogspot.com
http://www.amazon.com/dp/B0075440PA  ©J Howard 2012

©copyright J Howard 2013  Author & Photographer J Howard www.jackie666.blog.com

God Helps Those
Who Help
Themself
To
Everything
Jacqueline Howard 2017 Author& Photographer
www.lovechiald.blogspot.com
http://www.amazon.com/dp/B0075440PA  ©J Howard 2012

196

LOVE
THE
ONE
THAT
GIVES
A
DAMN
bY j hOWARD 2017
LOVECHIALD.BLOGSPOT.COM

On FunNY FARM
NO IFS
Just Butts
©copyright Jacqueline 2012   www.jackie666.blog.com

YAMAHA

Business Email Lovechiald@hotmail.com

Donations to:  PayPal.Me/lovechilds

Thank you for tuning in to my Book Titled 'Like Aliens Hitching a Ride on Human Brains'.  Author Jacqueline Howard 2018.

©Copyright Jacqueline Howard.

Photography by Jacqueline Howard ©Jacqueline Howard 2018.

202

Notes:

This page is for the readers who may wish to right in.

203

Notes:

www.ingramcontent.com/pod-product-compliance
Lightning Source LLC
Chambersburg PA
CBHW050808260726
48660CB00004B/1307